Picture credits:
l: Left, r: Right, t: Top, b: Bottom, c: Centre
Front Cover Images: Matthew Gough/Shutterstock: t, Gianna Stadelmyer/Shutterstock: c, Janne/Shutterstock: c, Wojciech/
shutterstock: ml, Andy Z./shutterstock: mc, Serghei Starus/Shutterstock: mr, Elisei Shafer/Shutterstock: b.

Back Cover Images: Carlos Arranz/Shutterstock: c, Maica/istock: mb.

Border Images: Galyna Andrushko/Shutterstock, Elisei Shafer/Shutterstock, Carlos Arranz/Shutterstock.

Insides: Nwinter/istock: 7tr, János Gehring/Shutterstock: 8c, Mikhail Olykainen/Shutterstock: 9tc, Matthew Gough/
Shutterstock: 9br, SilksAtSunrise/Shutterstock: 10tm, Vicki France/Dreamstime: 11br,
Paul Vorwerk/Shutterstock: 12bc, Fleyeing/Dreamstime: 13tl, oculo/Shutterstock: 13br, Condor 36/Shutterstock: 15tr,
Gumenuk Vitalij/Dreamstime: 15bm, Vova Pomortzeff/Shutterstock: 16cr, Sally Scott/Shutterstock: 17b,
Arlene Jean Gee/Shutterstock: 18-19c, Andy Z./Shutterstock: 19mr, JacobH/istock: 20m, justin maresch/Shutterstock: 21tr,
Jose Manuel Gelpi Diaz/Dreamstime: 21ml, Yvanovich/Dreamstime: 22tm, Stephen Meese/Shutterstock: 23tr,
Keith Levit/Shutterstock: 23bm, Stanislav Popov/istock: 24mr, Iouri Timofeev/Dreamstime: 24-25tc, brm1949/istock: 25br,
Ljupco Smokovski/Shutterstock: 26mr, Pedro Jorge Henriques Monteiro/Shutterstock: 26br, bevan young/istock: 27tc,
EcoPrint/Shutterstock: 28mc, Deborah Hewitt/Dreamstime: 29tl, tshortell/Redbugg Design/istock: 29br,
Rpsycho/istock: 30-31mc, glaflamme/istock: 31tr, Jose Gil/shutterstock: 32cr, Armin Rose/Shutterstock: 33tm,
Tonis Valing/Shutterstock: 33bl, Snowleopard1/Shutterstock: 35tl, Carolina Garcia Aranda/Dreamstime: 35mr, Ferdericb/
Dreamstime: 36bl, Starper/Dreamstime: 38cl, Kitch Bain/Shutterstock: 39tl,
vladyslav morozov/Shutterstock: 39b, Roca/Shutterstock: 40-41c, Condor 36/Shutterstock: 42lb,
Pierdelune/Shuttersock: 42-43tc, lloyd hess/istock:43tr, Rachelle Burnside/Shutterstock: 43bm.

ALL ILLUSTRATIONS MADE BY Q2A MEDIA

Published By: Robert Frederick Ltd.
4 North Parade Bath, England.

This Edition: 2021

Saving Planet Earth

CONTENTS

Threatened World	6
World Today	8
Burning Earth	10
The Problem with Oil	12
Wildlife Crisis	14
Something Fishy	16
Whales in Danger	18
Birds on the Brink	20
On the List	22
Heal the World	24
Turning Green	26
Big Help	28
Organic Advantages	30
Alternative Energy	32
Solar Energy	34
Water Power	36
Wind Energy	38
Hybrid and Electric Vehicles	40
Recycling	42
Making Anew	44

Threatened World

The Earth has gone through some major environmental changes over the centuries, attributable to natural causes. However, since the Industrial Revolution, a human impact upon the environment has become apparent.

Tree Times

Scientists believe the first plants grew in water. Then, about 500 million years ago, some of these small plants began to grow on land. The first trees on Earth took root nearly 460 million years ago. *Archaeopteris* was one of the earliest known modern trees on Earth. It is not found today because it became extinct many years ago. New forests grew in its place, but trees have never been under as much threat as they are today. They are being cut down for wood, to make way for new towns and roads and for farmers to grow more food to meet the growing number of people and cattle. Deforestation destroys the habitats of many plants, and animals.

ECO fact

The Endangered Species Act was passed in 1973 to help protect the world's most endangered plant and animal species.

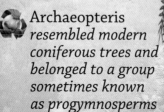 *Archaeopteris resembled modern coniferous trees and belonged to a group sometimes known as progymnosperms*

Blow Away the Clouds

Deforestation harms the climate. Trees let out large amounts of water vapour. This helps form new clouds. When trees are cut down, the land becomes dry. Moreover, trees help us by absorbing harmful gases, such as carbon dioxide, while making food through photosynthesis, and releasing oxygen.

The harmful effects of deforestation have to be stopped as soon as possible. Otherwise, by the year 2030 as much as 80 percent of the world's total forest area will have been destroyed

Where Did The Dodo Go?

Have you seen the dodo? None of us have. It was a bird that was last seen in 1662. The dodo could not fly and was hunted to extinction by humans and their dogs. While some people killed it for its meat, others killed it to preserve its head for religious ceremonies. Many animals are threatened with extinction because of human activity. Hacking down forests means robbing these animals of their homes.

The dodo was an unfortunate species of bird that became extinct as a direct consequence of human activity

The World Today

Trees are being cut down to make space for people to live and work

Our Earth has been around for billions of years. However, in the past 150 years, human activity has led to faster changes than the world has seen in thousands of years.

Trees, Please!

Land makes up only a third of the Earth's surface. Until a few hundred years ago, much of this land was covered with forest. In a forest, the trees are so close together that their crowns touch and look like one large canopy. But these forests have steadily been cut down for wood and to make more land available for roads, factories and towns.

Where's My Home?

Trees and forests are home to a vast variety of wildlife. If the rainforests were to disappear, almost half the world's plants and animals would lose their home. In order to run factories and produce more electricity, huge amounts of coal, oil, iron ore and other natural resources are being mined from inside the Earth. These are resources that take millions of years to form and we are losing them faster than the Earth can make them.

Phew, It's Hot!

Plants make food by taking in carbon dioxide—a gas that is harmful to us and causes global warming—and giving out oxygen. However, in the last hundred years or so, emissions from factories and vehicles, have been releasing more and more harmful gases, such as carbon dioxide. Cutting down trees disturbs the balance between oxygen and carbon dioxide in the air.

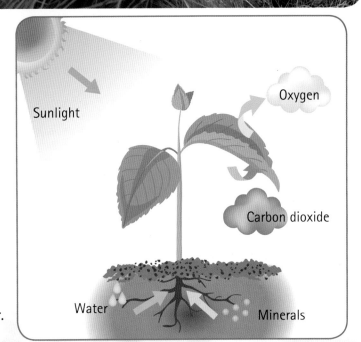

Sunlight

Oxygen

Carbon dioxide

Water

Minerals

 Plants make their food with the help of sunlight, carbon dioxide and water. This is known as photosynthesis

Many species of plants and animals are threatened with extinction because rainforests are being cut down

ECO fact

Many medicines prescribed by doctors are made from plants. Approximately one in four medicines is made using ingredients from rainforest trees.

Burning Earth

In the last hundred years or so, the Earth has become warmer and warmer. This process is known as global warming.

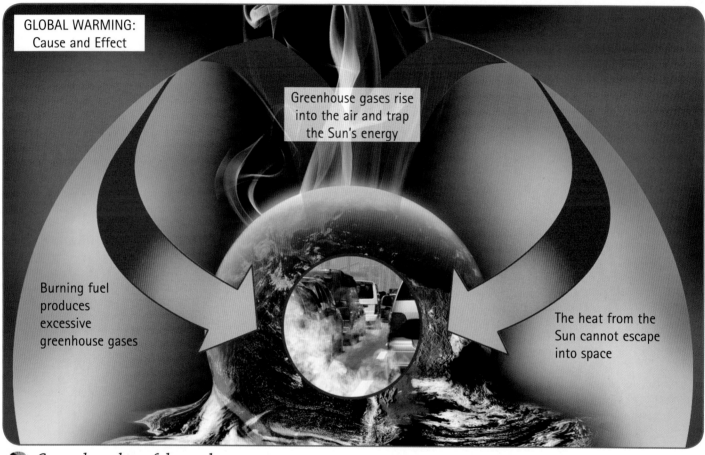

GLOBAL WARMING:
Cause and Effect

Greenhouse gases rise into the air and trap the Sun's energy

Burning fuel produces excessive greenhouse gases

The heat from the Sun cannot escape into space

 Cars release harmful greenhouse gases that contribute to global warming

Who Turned On the Heat?

Scientists are still studying the sudden rise in the Earth's temperature and most agree it is because of the way we live and work today. Greenhouse gases such as carbon dioxide, that trap the Sun's heat, are a major cause of global warming. These gases are released mainly by vehicles and factories.

Fiery Cycle

Global warming seems to have led to more extreme weather around the world. There are more fierce storms than ever before. The El Nino southern oscillation is a global phenomenon that takes place in the ocean-atmosphere. These conditions have led to extremely dry weather conditions and severe bush fires in places like Australia. The forest fires burn down trees and release massive amounts of carbon dioxide.

Melting Globe

The world is getting warmer. Mountain glaciers are melting and so is ice in the Polar regions. In 2006, Greenland saw more days of snowmelt than it had in 18 years. Wet, melting snow absorbs more of the Sun's energy than dry snow. Dry snow reflects most of this energy. The more the glaciers melt the more water flows into rivers, lakes and seas, raising the level of water and leading to terrible floods.

Glaciers feed thousands of rivers. But too much water causes floods

ECO fact

Today, the world's atmosphere has about twice as much carbon dioxide than there was at the start of the Industrial Revolution.

With temperatures rising around the world destructive forest fires are seen often

The Problem with Oil

Oil spills are a recent human-made disaster that affect thousands of marine and land animals. The earliest known oil well was drilled in China around 347 B.C.

Tankers carry large amounts of oil that can be spilled if the tanker struggles during extremely bad weather

SAFETY FIRST

NO SMOKING

Going Places

Crude oil has to be carried from where it is found to where it is needed. Even refined petroleum products like diesel and petrol have to be transported. Sometimes, some of the oil is spilled by accident. Tanker ships carry so much oil that one accident can release millions of gallons of oil.

ECO fact

On 11 February 1993, about 30,000 birds died because of an oil spill from a passing ship.

The Torrey Canyon *incident spilled around 132,277 tons of crude oil that caused a lot of damage*

On Land, Too

Oil spills on land happen around oil wells. They pollute the surrounding soil and seep into the ground, where the oil can enter the water table. Spills take months and sometimes even years to clean up. Oil poisons birds and chokes and poisons plants and animals that live in water. If the spill is near the shore, beaches get polluted.

Going On For Decades

One of the earliest oil spills was in 1967, when the *Torrey Canyon* ran aground near Cornwall, England. On March 16, 1978, the *Amoco Cadiz* spilled about 1.6 million barrels of crude oil near France. On August 6, 1983, the tanker *Castillo de Bellver* caught fire near Cape Town in South Africa.

Oil spills on water can be more easily seen

Wildlife Crisis

Just a quarter of the surface of this Earth is dry land.
There should be enough space for animals and humans to live
happily side by side, but unfortunately this isn't always the case.

Vaccines develop immunity to targeted diseases

Where's My Home Gone?

Improvements and progress in medical science have increased the life span of humans. Children are increasingly protected from deadly diseases through inoculations. This means there are more people on Earth than ever before. The battle for space between animals and humans is on. Changing weather brings with it new problems. The world is becoming warmer. Bugs just love that! Most bacteria cannot live in the cold and fare much better in the heat. They are invading new places that are now warm enough for them to live in. Due to global warming, a fungal disease has killed a large number of frogs across the world.

ECO fact

Polar bears in the Hudson Bay sleep through six to eight months of summer. They wake up in winter and hunt for food. Global warming means longer summers and weaker polar bears. Weaker mothers have 15 percent fewer cubs.

Your Food or Mine?

Forests that are home to wild animals, such as bears, tigers, leopards, elephants and thousands of smaller creatures, are being cleared to make homes for humans. Land is also needed to plant crops for our food and for infrastructure like railway lines, airports and factories. To power all this we need fuel, resulting in the digging of mines and wells. This destruction of the natural habitat is leading to a rapid decrease in the number of animals in the world.

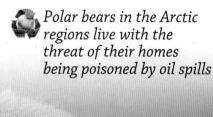

Animals live and survive in forests. With forests being cleared, these creatures are left homeless

Push the Polar Bear

The search for more crude oil has reached the Chukchi Sea in Alaska. Land is being leased out to companies that are trying to find oil and gas. Even if they drill for oil offshore, the results will be seen for miles around with more roads, towns, traffic, noise and other pollution. If oil from the well spills out, it will poison the waters around. This in turn will affect polar bears and other Arctic wildlife.

Polar bears in the Arctic regions live with the threat of their homes being poisoned by oil spills

Something Fishy

Fish provide food and nutrition for millions of people around the world. In some cultures fish constitutes the majority of the diet. In other cultures fish is much less of a staple.

A Little Too Much Fish

Fish is a healthy source of food, since it is rich in fatty acids and proteins. In many parts of the world people still regularly fish on a small scale to feed their families. But the population of the world is growing so fast that fishing methods are changing rapidly. Overfishing has become a big problem around the world as larger fishing vessels with bigger nets trawl the seas. Worldwide, legislation surrounding fishing rights and quotas is extremely complicated. Much of the legislation is designed to protect stock levels.

ECO fact

Commercial trawlers drag nets along the bottom of the sea. These nets are criticised for damaging the seabed and for catching everything in their way.

In some parts of the world people regularly fish for themselves

Modern Methods

Fishing fleets use the latest methods to maximise their catch each time a trawler goes out. As the trawler net is dragged it scoops up anything in its path that isn't small enough to fit between the netting. Critics argue that this leads to many fish being caught that will just be thrown back, either because they're an unsuitable species, or because they're too small.

No Time to Grow

Before the days of trawler fishing, fishermen were sensitive of the breeding seasons and would often not catch certain fish during certain months. But this traditional method of fishing is decreasing. Now, fishing fleets fish year round, so sensitive breeding cycles are often interrupted.

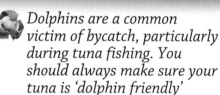

Dolphins are a common victim of bycatch, particularly during tuna fishing. You should always make sure your tuna is 'dolphin friendly'

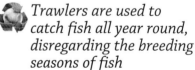

Trawlers are used to catch fish all year round, disregarding the breeding seasons of fish

Whales in Danger

Whales are among the largest living creatures in the world. Blue whales are the largest mammals. But even they are not safe anymore. Most of the danger to them comes from humans.

Unsafe Seas

The world's rivers empty out into the seas. In some parts of the world chemicals from factories and sewage from homes is emptied into rivers without being treated properly. Sometimes, rivers are polluted by accidental spills. This pollution can find its way downstream and eventually empty out into the seas.

No Fault of Theirs

Thousands of whales have been killed over the years for food and oil. This is known as whaling. As many as five out of the thirteen species of great whales are now endangered as a result of excessive whaling. While most countries have put a stop to this practice, there are still some countries, such as Japan, Greenland and the Faroe Islands, that still allow whaling. Pressure groups are increasingly targeting whaling vessels in their protests.

 Explosive harpoons are used to catch whales at sea while whaling

Many whale species, including blue whales, fin whales and right whales, are endangered due to human activity

Many parts of the whale are processed for commercial use. Even its teeth and bones are used for decorative articles

Killed for Greed

Whaling dates back to as early as 6000 B.C. Modern whaling techniques kill more whales than ever before. In an effort to decrease the amount of commercial whaling and prevent the extinction of certain whale species, the International Whaling Commission (IWC) passed a ban on commercial whaling in 1986. However, the demand for whale blubber has increased over the last 100 years. Whale oils are also very popular. Apart from the blubber and oil, their bones are also traded. Whales have a relatively long gestation period and can take years to reach maturity. This means that many species are dropping in number as not enough babies reach maturity to reproduce.

ECO fact

The grey whale is extinct while the beluga and bowhead whales are critically endangered. However, whale meat is not very safe for consumption. This is because it contains high levels of dangerous toxins.

Birds on the Brink

Birds are found in almost every part of the world. Some fly, others swim! While some birds live in one place most of their life, others migrate over enormous distances. Many species of birds are threatened by human activity.

 Soil that doesn't contain enough organic matter can be made more fertile by adding guano to it

Do We Need Birds?

Birds are not just our pretty, feathered friends. They actually help us too. Some birds eat insects that harm crops. Birds that feed on nectar help to pollinate flowers. Those who eat fruit scatter the seeds far and wide and help grow new plants and trees. Bird droppings, or guano, is also an important fertiliser in some parts of the world.

ECO fact

In November 2007, more than 30,000 birds died from an oil spill in the Black Sea from a leak in an oil tanker.

Penguins are dying because their homes are melting away and taking away their food

On a Wing and a Prayer

Many birds that were once abundant are not to be found anymore. When people started inhabiting the Polynesian, Melanesian and Micronesian islands, about 750 to 1800 species of birds became extinct. Birds that like cold climates, such as penguins, could become increasingly threatened because of global warming. In the Antarctic, penguins feed on krill, which feed on algae that collects on the ice. Now, with less ice, there is less algae, so there is less krill for penguins to feed on.

Falling Everywhere

Many birds that were common even a few years ago have almost disappeared. The house sparrow and vulture are seldom sighted in places where they were common. According to the Red List, more than 1,200 species of birds are believed to be threatened or in danger of being wiped out. One major reason is the decrease of forests, shrubland, and grassland where they live and forage for food. Birds have also decreased due to hunting. Some pesticides used by farmers can also pose a threat to birds.

Some birds migrate several thousand miles each year

On the List

The Tasmanian wolf has been extinct for approximately 65 years. The English wolf has also become extinct. With current trends many more species of animals might also soon become extinct.

What's This List?

Groups of people have been trying to save plants and animals for future generations. The International Union for the Conservation of Nature and Natural Resources (IUCN) is a group that works to save our natural world. The IUCN Red List of Threatened Species was first published in 1963. It is also known as the IUCN Red List. It is the most important and detailed list of threatened and endangered plants and animals across the world. By looking at the IUCN Red List, governments, organisations and people around the world know the status of each species of animal in the world. There are nine groups in the list:

- Not Evaluated (those that have not yet been studied)
- Data Deficient (those for which there is not enough information)
- Least Concern (such as rock pigeons and snail kites)
- Near Threatened (such as leafy sea dragons)
- Vulnerable (such as wild goats and yaks)
- Endangered (such as blue whales)
- Critically Endangered (such as the Javan rhino)
- Extinct in the Wild (but found in captivity)
- Extinct (such as dodos and thylacines)

ECO fact

The latest Red List has the names of 19,817 species that are threatened with extinction, 3,947 critically endangered, and 5,766 as endangered, while more than 10,000 are listed as vulnerable.

The Tasmanian wolf was found in Australia and New Guinea, and became extinct during the 1900s

One Happy Family

The IUCN list is drawn up after analyzing reports submitted by many organizations from across the world. These include the Zoological Society of London's Institute of Zoology, the Species Survival Commission, and Bird Life International. The IUCN aims to re-evaluate every category of species in the world every five years or at least every 10 years to ascertain its status in the natural world.

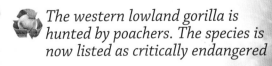

The Bornean orangutan can be found on the island of Borneo. One of the greatest threats to its survival is the bushmeat trade

The Latest List

The lastest list of threatened species was released by the IUCN in July 2012. Overfishing has pushed two families of rays to the brink of extinction, while hunting and habitat loss have led to the decline of seven primate species. The update also reveals further evidence of the perilous state of freshwater fish globally.

The western lowland gorilla is hunted by poachers. The species is now listed as critically endangered

Heal the World

Many groups around the world work to try to save the planet. Some are local groups, while others are worldwide organisations.

IUCN

The International Union for the Conservation of Nature and Natural Resources is the largest organisation of its kind and works with hundreds of governments and international organisations. The Red List gives the status of plants and animals around the world.

ECO fact

The International Fund for Animal Welfare (IFAW), tries to prevent cruelty to animals, protects wildlife and rescues animals.

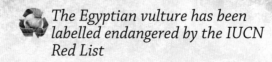
The Egyptian vulture has been labelled endangered by the IUCN Red List

WWF

The World Wildlife Fund for Nature (WWF) was started in 1961. It is one of the largest independent environmental organisations in the world and works in more than 90 countries. It is working on more than 15,000 conservation and environmental projects all over the world, which try to safeguard the security of thousands of endangered species.

The WWF adopted the giant panda as its logo

By the Law

Animals and plants don't have artificial borders. So we have to work together to save them. World leaders are also trying to come together for a solution to save the world. One such step is the organisation of CITES, or the Convention on International Trade in Endangered Species of Wild Fauna and Flora. It was drafted at the 1963 meeting of the IUCN and came into force in July 1975. It is an international agreement between governments. It tries to control trade in animals and plants, prevent poaching and limit the destruction of forests and oceans.

CITES helps governments to protect more than 30,000 species of animals and plants

Turning Green

The effects of deforestation have begun to show. Scientists, governments, and advocacy groups have realised that it is time to plant trees.

We Gain Again!

Trees can be planted in open land that had once been a forest. This is called afforestation. Planting trees in areas where forests are thinning out but still stand is known as reforestation. Once the trees grow, their roots hold the soil together and they begin to absorb carbon dioxide and release oxygen into the air. Trees give us many other benefits. People in many countries eat off plates made out of broad leaves. They also give us products like rubber and timber, as long as other trees are planted.

ECO fact

The reforestation efforts in Tillamook Burn took off only when large groups of people came forward to plant more than 72 million seedlings.

Reforestation is an effective way of bringing back life into areas affected by deforestation

Mangrove trees can grow in regions that are extremely salty

Only by planting new trees can forests be saved from dying out

Stop the Sea!

When storms lash the land, the coasts are hit hard. Most of the destruction during the Indian Ocean tsunami of 2004 was along coastal areas. Large areas of land was washed away and people suddenly found the ground on which they lived underwater. Afforestation has begun in countries like India, Bangladesh, Malaysia, China and Indonesia. Mangrove trees are being planted in the low-lying coastal and salty regions to hold the soil together. Bangladesh has planted over 113,000 hectares of mangrove trees since 1966.

China Trees

In May 2002, China began the world's largest reforestation project. This was necessary because trees had been cut for decades and huge areas of the country were turning bare. Forests can be planted even after the earlier trees have been burned down. The Tillamook Burn in Oregon, for example, broke out on August 14, 1933, and then in 1939, 1945 and 1951. The 1951 fire destroyed 32,700 acres. Reforestation began in this area in 1945, covering around 300,000 acres of land.

Big Help

Trees help us in many ways and their benefits extend far beyond their impact on climate.

Hold the Soil

Tree roots hold the soil together and protect it from being washed away by heavy rain. The topsoil is extremely precious, as it takes between 100-500 years for an inch to form, depending on the climate and type of rock. When this soil is washed away, it settles in riverbeds and lakes as silt. This reduces the amount of water these rivers can hold and also causes floods. In the hills, roots of trees prevent the soil and rocks from slipping downhill as landslides.

Leaves of trees form an umbrella over the land and break the force of rainwater that can wash away soil

Trees provide a safe refuge for birds so that they may build their nests, lay eggs and keep their chicks warm

Natural Coolers

Trees absorb carbon dioxide, keeping the air cool and clean. Leaves clean the air by absorbing dust and other harmful particles. During the day, they release oxygen, which we breathe. They also release water vapour into the air. These droplets of vapour form clouds and bring us rain. Trees are a natural home for millions of animals. They also help to break the speed of wind. This stops the spread of deserts (desertification).

ECO fact

One tree can absorb as much carbon in a year as a car produces while driving 26,000 miles.

A single tree produces approximately 260 pounds of oxygen per year.

Other Uses

Trees have many other uses and their parts are used in different ways. Medicines are made from their bark, leaves, fruit, flowers and roots. Tree houses are home to people who live in forests. Many products, such as cosmetics, are also made from trees.

Wooden tree houses fascinate and provide adventure to both children and adults

Organic Advantages

Chemical fertilisers were first used in the 19th century. However, when their harmful effects became obvious, the organic movement started.

What Is Organic Farming?

Organic farming uses only natural fertilisers, such as manure, and natural pesticides. No chemical fertilisers or pesticides are used. Moreover, instead of growing just one crop, organic farmers rotate crops, growing different plants on one farm, to discourage pests and loss of the nutrient value of the soil. Food that has been grown according to the methods laid down by the International Federation of Organic Agriculture Movements carries the organic label.

Back to the Roots

The Green Revolution introduced monoculture, or growing only one kind of crop for higher yield. As a result, many types of seeds were lost. But, during the organic movement, new seed banks were set up to collect wild and local seeds. Traditional ways of growing crops were also slowly re-introduced. Farmers in some places returned to organic farming, using natural fertilisers and pesticides.

The organic movement has made organic foods increasingly popular

Eat Organic

We can take in tiny amounts of pesticides when we eat crops that have been sprayed. Pesticide residues are found in all kinds of food, from fruit to milk and even baby food. But organic farms do not use chemical fertilisers. Animals brought up on an organic farm are not fed growth hormones to grow faster. Organic foods are rich in vitamins and minerals. They are considered by many to taste better too. However, organic food does come at a premium in price.

 The organic movement encourages the use of traditional and natural fertilisers, such as manure

Arround 310,000 square kilometres (75 million acres) of land is under organic farming

ECO fact

The United Kingdom uses about 31,000 tonnes (34,171 tons) of pesticides every year.

Alternative Energy

The demand for energy is growing. The constant increase in population is leading to the use of more cars and electricity. The constant use of different sources of energy leads to more pollution and the fear of its depletion.

What Most of us Use

Most vehicles run on fossil fuels. These include coal, petroleum and natural gas. These fuels take millions of years to form. Continuous and extensive use of such fossil fuels will eventually lead to their depletion. Fossil fuels also cause a lot of pollution. They lead to more greenhouse gases and cause global warming. Nuclear power, a recent source of energy, is harmful because of the dangerous radioactive waste it produces. Thus, there is now a search for alternative fuels. These include renewable sources of energy such as the Sun, the wind and even waves.

> ### ECO fact
> Oil constitutes about 40 per cent of the world's commercial energy. Transport, in the form of road, rail, air and water uses 60 per cent of the total oil produced.

Alternative Energy to the Rescue?

Energy from alternative sources can be put to several uses. Solar energy can be used as a source of electricity, and heat. Wind energy can produce electricity, grind grain and run pumps to drain out water. Energy from waves can be used to generate electricity and pump water. Energy from biomass, which includes crop waste, grass and husks of grain, can be used in factories. Energy from biomass can even be used to light up homes and villages and for cooking.

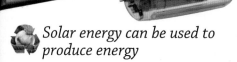
Solar energy can be used to produce energy

Tidal wave turbines harvest electricity from the ocean tides

Cleaner Fuel

Alternative fuels, such as solar, wave and wind energy, are renewable. Sources of fuel, such as biomass, are cheaper than petroleum and other fossil fuels. They are also safer than nuclear power. An accidental leak from a nuclear power station can cause a huge disaster. For instance, on 26 April, 1986, the Chernobyl nuclear power plant in the Ukraine exploded and caused the deaths of 57 people. The ongoing impact of the radiation in the region is still being felt to this day and has caused the deaths of many more.

Nuclear power plants are a contentious form of energy supply

Geothermal energy is free of pollutants and renewable

Energy from Heat

Geothermal energy is harvested from the heat stored inside the Earth's surface formed by the decay of plants and minerals buried millions of years ago. Even though it was originally used only for heating water, today it is used for generating electricity. It is renewable, pollution-free and reliable, but it cannot be generated everywhere. Currently, geothermal energy is harvested for electricity only along tectonic boundaries. The energy is tapped by drilling wells into underground hot water reservoirs. A few geothermal plants directly use the steam to power a generator or turbine. Others use the hot water to boil another liquid, which in turn vapourizes and causes the turbine to spin.

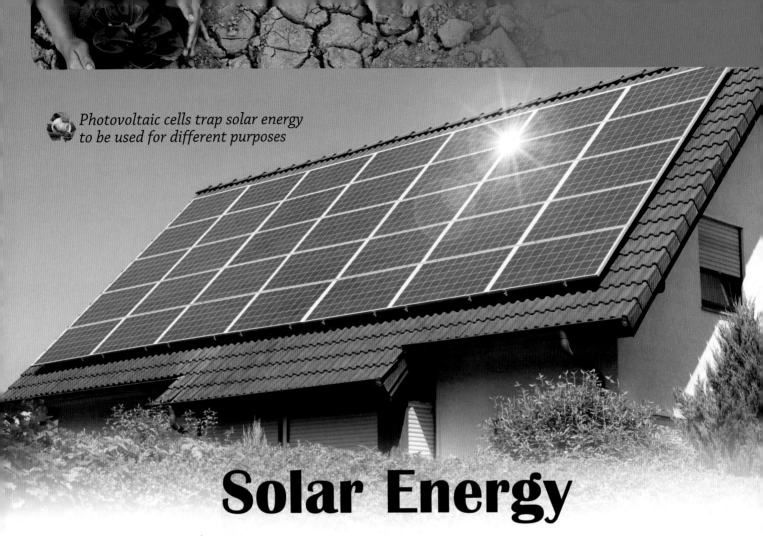

Photovoltaic cells trap solar energy to be used for different purposes

Solar Energy

Without the Sun there would be no life on Earth. Solar power is an alternative source of energy that is being increasingly used in many parts of the world. It is a safe and clean source, and there is no fear of it ever running out!

Shining Bright

Solar energy can be put to a number of uses. Energy from the Sun can light up our homes, streets and offices. Several cities use solar energy to power traffic lights. For centuries, people in cold places have built their homes to face the Sun. Modern technology can convert sunlight into electricity through photovoltaic cells or by heating a liquid that runs a generator through steam. It is used to heat water and warm rooms, and even to cook food by the same process as an electric oven. Solar energy can also be used in household activities, such as ironing.

Warming Up

Energy from the Sun is used to heat spaces and to keep rooms ventilated. It is used in industries and to distil and disinfect water. Solar cookers are used for cooking food. It can even be used to pasteurise milk.

 *Solar cookers convert solar energy into heat to cook food*

Revving Up with the Sun

Solar vehicles are powered by the Sun's energy, which is trapped by panels on the cars. These photovoltaic, or PV, cells turn the Sun's energy into electrical energy that powers the car. There are at least two car races only for vehicles that run on solar energy: the World Solar Challenge and the North American Solar Challenge, both held in the United States.

Several concept cars are now being manufactured that use solar energy

ECO fact

Bysanivaripalle is the first village of its kind in India to use only solar cookers! Every home in the village has been cooking with solar since 2004.

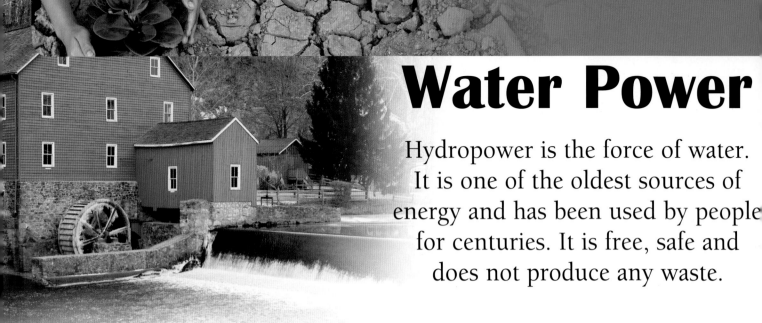

Water Power

Hydropower is the force of water. It is one of the oldest sources of energy and has been used by people for centuries. It is free, safe and does not produce any waste.

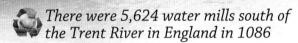

There were 5,624 water mills south of the Trent River in England in 1086

In the Past

Hydropower is one of the largest renewable sources of energy. Water power has been used for many years to move wheels attached to a grinder to grind corn or wheat. The wheels were often placed in the middle of the river, which turned with the flow of the river water. These were known as water mills.

Types of Water Power

Tidal energy is a form of hydropower that uses tidal currents in water to generate energy. The water turns turbines that convert the energy into electricity. As two thirds of the world is covered with water, the potential energy of the sea is enormous. However, there are significant costs and risks involved, as well as potential environmental impacts.

Light in Our Lives

One of the most important uses of hydropower is to produce electricity. In most countries, large dams are built across rivers to hold water. This water turns turbines, which convert the energy into electricity. Hydro-electric energy is cleaner and cheaper than energy produced by burning fossil fuels. However, the construction of large dams and power plants on rivers harms fish and other water creatures that live there. Dams often involve the displacement of large numbers of the population, as people are moved to make way for the large flooded areas that are to be created.

Tidal power stations convert tidal energy into electrical energy and other forms of energy

ECO fact

Hydropower is the world's largest source of renewable energy and constitutes about 7 percent of the total energy worldwide.

Large dams built across rivers harness the energy from the water. This energy is safe, clean and renewable, but does come with its own environmental impact

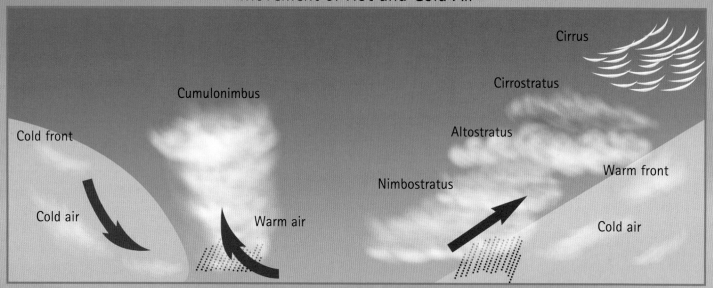

Cirrus

Cirrostratus

Cumulonimbus

Altostratus

Cold front

Nimbostratus

Warm front

Cold air

Warm air

Cold air

Wind Energy

For thousands of years, people have used the power of wind to their advantage. Wind power is the conversion of wind energy into other forms of energy, such as electricity.

Blow, Wind, Blow!

The wind blows because of the Sun. Heat from the Sun warms the air. Hot air rises and cool air rushes in to fill the space. Since the entire world cannot be heated evenly at the same time by the Sun, the wind is always blowing. This wind energy can produce electricity, grind grain and run pumps.

The Miller's Best Friend

Early windmills used wind energy to turn their sails. Windmills turn the wind's kinetic energy into mechanical energy. Modern wind turbines turn this kinetic energy into electrical energy. These modern windmills or wind turbines may not look much like the windmills that ground corn, but most of them still use two or three blades to catch the wind's energy.

Wind-powered generators throughout the world produced 591.5 gigawatts of energy by the end of 2018

ECO fact

According to scientists, the best places in the world to generate wind power are in northern Europe, the southern tip of South America, Tasmania and the Great Lakes region in the United States.

One Windy Day

Wind blows throughout the day and night, but it has hardly been used to produce electricity in recent years. Countries have not used wind energy as much as they could. Just 1 percent of the total electricity in the world comes from wind energy. Wind is a free source of energy, which is clean and does not cause pollution. However, no one has yet been able to predict how much wind will blow at a given time, and so, it is an uncertain source of energy.

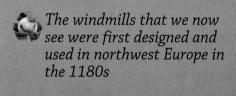

The windmills that we now see were first designed and used in northwest Europe in the 1180s

Hybrid and Electric Vehicles

With a diminishing supply of fossil fuels, increasing oil prices, pollution and greenhouse gas emissions resulting from its use, people are switching to cleaner and more efficient means of transportation like hybrid vehicles and electric cars.

Why Are Hybrids Important?

Hybrid vehicles take the best advantage of different fuels. For instance, a hybrid electric car has the efficiency of an internal combustion gasoline engine and the electric motor that can save fuel and increase power. Some hybrid vehicles save gasoline by shutting off the engine when the vehicle stops. These vehicles are powered by methanol or ethanol derived from agricultural crops and waste materials. Large vehicles such as trains can also be hybrid. These trains run on electric and diesel engines.

Electric Vehicles on the Go

An electric car is a vehicle with one or more motors powered by rechargeable batteries. It is energy efficient, and low in noise and emissions – not surprisingly, the sales of electric cars have been rising steadily.

Hybrid vehicles are less noisy than single-energy vehicles

ECO fact

There are more than 30 different models of electric vehicles available. The Nissan Leaf and Tesla Model S are the most popular electric cars.

Tesla's Electric Car Revolution

Tesla Inc. is an American technology company that specializes in electric cars and rechargeable batteries for these cars. It was named after the famous scientist Nikolas Tesla. The three models manufactured here are Model S, Model X, and Model 3.

The car's battery can be recharged at specific refill points on the streets or at home by plugging it into the power socket. The company has started developing 'supercharger' stations in different locations to quickly recharge the car for long-distance trips.

What's Up at the Gigafactory?

The Gigafactory is a production plant that manufactures the batteries and battery packs for these vehicles. Electric vehicles will be the future of transportation and will likely be the norm in the decades to come.

Many countries are already investing in research and development of better and more innovative electric vehicles to address future needs of clean, affordable, and smart modes of transportation.

Recycling

Recycling is the process of reusing something after its first use is over. Recycled things are often used in a new way. If your shoelaces begin to fray, you can recycle them by tying them up in knots to make a key chain. Old things are recycled in factories to make something new.

Why Recycle?

Many cities are running short of land for landfill. This means there is too much rubbish and too little space to keep it in. Rubbish rots and can smell. Landfills look ugly and can poison the land and water around them. When you recycle something, you are easing the pressure on landfill. An added benefit is that the need for the mining for more aluminium for new cans is reduced; this saves time and energy and reduces the emissions of greenhouse gases.

The more we throw away, the bigger our landfills grow

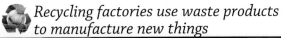
Compost provides important nutrients on which plants thrive

Recycling factories use waste products to manufacture new things

What Can Be recycled?

Recycling begins with separating things that can be recycled and then having them collected for recycling. Paper, plastic, metal, glass, rubber, cardboard, and cloth, can all be recycled. The recycled product can be the same as the original item, like an aluminium can, or it can be something very different. Even leftover food can be recycled. Rather than throwing it in the bin, kitchen waste like vegetable peel can be kept in a closed container, mixed with soil and garden waste. In a matter of months, this mixture turns into compost, which is a type of fertiliser that helps plants to grow.

Each of Us Can Pitch In

Recycling is a way of managing and reducing waste. Waste management begins at the time we buy something. If we buy only what we need, then we have less to throw away. As a society we are very wasteful. Before you throw something away, think if it can be used again, recycled, or made into compost. In this way each one of us can help to reduce the amount of waste we produce.

Making Anew

Anything biodegradable can be broken down into raw form with the help of bacteria and other living organisms, such as worms.

Wood Forever

Small pieces of timber waste need not be thrown out. They can be recycled and made into useful things. Reusing wood from old furniture and old buildings is a simple way to fit the old into a new place. Wood that cannot be saved or has broken into small pieces is recycled by putting it through the mill again. Poor-quality wood can be made into mulch and laid out over banks to stop soil from being washed away. If the wood cannot be used in any of these ways, it can be used as fuel in factories or in homes.

Pulp to Paper to Pulp

Over 40 percent of the wood that is cut down is made into paper. It can be recycled and made into new things, including new paper. No piece of paper is too small to be recycled. The paper is first made into pulp by adding water. It is then beaten to separate fibres and then put through a screen to filter out larger pieces. The pulp is kneaded and bleached and made into paper. Recycling a ton of paper saves at least that amount, or more, of wood.

Re-milled timber is often made into timber flooring and other products

ECO fact

The Ecopod is a coffin made by a manufacturer in the United Kingdom. It is made from paper pulp from recycled paper that hardens into a biodegradable box.

Paper pulp is used to make new paper from used paper

Earth to Earth

Biodegradable waste, including animal and human waste, can be composted. It is decomposed by bacteria and fungi and insects like ants and earthworms. Large amounts of biodegradable waste can be turned into biogas, which is a renewable source of energy.

Biodegradable waste can be composted at home in a compost bin